BECOMING THE ELEPHANT
IN THE ROOM

JUSTIN MOORE
FOUNDER OF THE ELEPHANT IN THE ROOM EXPERIENCE WITH
CLAY CLARK
U.S. SMALL BUSINESS ADMINISTRATION
ENTREPRENEUR OF THE YEAR

Becoming the Elephant in the Room:
57 Words of Wisdom & Mindsets to Becoming a Successful Person

ISBN 978-0-9998649-2-0

Copyright © 2018 by Brian and Jessi Gibson

Thrive Publishing

Published by Thrive Publishing
1100 Suite #100 Riverwalk Terrace
Jenks, OK 74037

Thrive Publishing books may be purchased for educational, business or sales promotional use. For more information, please email the Special Markets Department at info@Thrive15.com. When crossing the street, please look both ways and do not stop, drop, and roll.

"Yes, Justin Moore is my brother-in-law, but that is not what I respect about him. I respect Justin's coachability at a time in his life when most would have quit. I respect Justin because he chose to shadow me for two years to master the art of "rising and grinding" every day at 4:00 AM while learning the diligence it requires to become a successful entrepreneur. I respect Justin for learning through osmosis that most ideas don't matter and that it's the execution of those ideas that matter most. I respect Justin because while the world was sleeping, Facebooking, drifting or complaining he was busy turning his dreams into reality. I'm excited for you to learn how the Elephant In The Room Men's Grooming Lounge phenomenon was started and I'm excited for those who have chosen to franchise with us to grow this wonderful brand throughout the country. I'm honored to serve you, the customer because without you there would be no business, no story, and no book. I'm sure this book will just the first of many for Justin, but I don't want to miss this opportunity to say here and now that I am proud of his work ethic and the brand we've built together."

– CLAY CLARK

(Former U.S. Small Business Administration Entrepreneur of the Year, the Co-Founder of The Elephant In The Room, Member of the Forbes Business Coach Council, and the host of iTunes chart-topping podcast, the Thrivetime Show)

WE ALL HAVE TO START SOMEWHERE
by Justin Moore (Co-Founder of Elephant In The Room)

We all have a story and I believe our stories need to be shared. Our stories can encourage, motivate, inspire and even challenge others to be their best. In this book, I share impactful principles and guidelines that I have personally learned through trial and error and the priceless lessons that have been taught to me directly by mentors (Clay Clark and others).

To fully understand my journey I want to first give you a glimpse into my childhood and the environment that I grew up in. It's important to know my back story because events from our childhood shape us into the people that we become as adults. You and I must realize that although negative events and experiences may have shaped us into who we are today, we absolutely do have the power to change. As for me, I did not begin to take control of my life until the age of 26.

AT THE BOTTOM

I vividly remember the day my mindset changed. I was at a loss. I had no career. My pursuit of professional baseball had officially ended way before I had anticipated and I felt I had no other talents to offer the world. I was financially, emotionally, and spirituality at the lowest point of my life. I was broke and living with my sister (Vanessa) and brother-in-law (Clay) after having just ended a failed 7-year relationship with my ex-wife.

CAUSE AND EFFECT

As I thought about where I was in life I realized that I was defining myself entirely based on the past events that had created my current financial, relationship and professional status. I was not able to define myself based on where I was going. After much soul-searching, I soon realized that dwelling on the failures of my past was not helping me to become the person I wanted to be in the future.

Want to own your own business? Learn more about franchise opportunities at www.EITRLounge.com

5

However, once I realized that every decision, every action and every choice I had made previously had gotten me to that exact reality I realized that I also had the power to make new choices and to make better decisions that would then, in turn, cause me to produce new results.

TAKING SMALL STEPS FORWARD

Rather than investing my days lamenting my current situation, I decided to focus on making positive daily decisions while taking daily positive action steps. I resolved in my mind that I could succeed if I just stayed focus on taking daily small and positive action steps like I had seen Clay do over the years. At that moment my journey towards success began. The seed was planted. I did not realize it at the time but this journey towards success would take me nearly six years of rising and grinding and working through adversity, trials and tribulations. One thing I did know is that things that were happening to me below the surface were making the difference. My mindset had now changed and it finally occurred to me that the only thing standing in the way of the achievement of my dreams was me.

MY DILIGENT DAD

My father was an extremely hard worker, and I know that I learned my hard work ethic from him. One thing I always remember him saying is "wherever you are working, whatever job you are doing, you better pay attention to every detail because you don't know what skill you will need to carry with you to the next job."

My Dad's career path did not involve following his passion, but it did involve supporting our family which both my sister and I appreciated. He found himself in a job that ended up becoming a career not because he loved it but because he now had a family to was providing for. I don't ever remember my Dad calling in sick or complaining about working overtime or working the night shifts that he did all throughout my childhood.

GROWING UP IN THE MIDDLE OF A 17 YEAR FIGHT

My mother was loving and caring and always wanted the best for me and Vanessa (my sister) and she helped me to realize the importance of showing your children loving care. As a young kid, I quickly observed that even though my parents were great people and had amazing qualities the combination of them both created a perpetually toxic environment. They fought with each other and fought to keep the marriage together until I was 17 years old. During those 17 years, they almost never stopped fighting. Our house was filled with verbal and physical violence on a daily basis. I vividly remember coming home from school and having the police at my house trying to help my Mom and Dad sort out their most recent out of control domestic dispute. The school bus driver was nice enough to drop me off at another kids' house, but it was visible to all the kids on the bus that there were 3 to 4 coup cars at the end of our street. To other kids, this was not normal and they wondered what was going on, but to me this was normal and I knew exactly what was going on.

GROWING UP IN A TOXIC ENVIRONMENT

Every day that I came home from school, I always wanted to be anywhere but at home. But when I was at home I was always worried that the bank was going to kick us out of our home again. I always worried about whether the repo men were going to take away our cars or our furniture again. As a kid I wasn't sure how I was going to succeed, but I did know that I never wanted to find myself living in either financial and relational bondage. However, little did I know that I was becoming a little more like my Mom and Dad with each passing year as I unintentionally allowed my environment to shape my personality, my expectations, and my sense of normal. I was becoming a product of my environment and I was headed down the on the same tracks they went down although I thought and said I wanted a different life.

Growing up in this daily toxic environment it impacted my sister and I. Because of the environment that we were raised in I tried to become a "peacekeeper"

Want to own your own business? Learn more about franchise opportunities at www.EITRLounge.com

7

and to be invisible. I simply could not handle any disagreement, and I didn't know how to resolve conflicts without them escalating.

I like the way my life was turning out, but I didn't know how to change myself until I faced the reality that as a man I had simply become a bi-product of my environment instead of living a purposeful and intentional life. I had not learned how to train my subconscious mind so that when life's decision points appeared I would make good decisions.

I soon realized that I wasn't meant to be a people pleaser and I started writing in a journal while living with Clay and Vanessa.

While living with my sister three power things occurred:

- I realized who I was and that it was up to me to build my character and my reputation.

- I realized that I wanted to be a source of motivational, inspiration and education for others.

- I realized the power of mentorship and coaching as a shadowed Clay on a daily basis.

For one of the first times in my life, I felt like I was now on the right track and that I could control the outcome. I knew this journey of intentional inspired living was going to be harder than anything I had previously done. I knew this journey would test me. I knew this journey would challenge me but I also knew that the personal growth that I would do on this journey was not going to be found only at the finish line. I knew that the character I had to develop and the person I would have to become to achieve the success I wanted was what this race was really all about. I knew that my success of failure was going to come down to the small decisions and action steps that I had to take on a daily basis.

I knew in order to become a source of motivation, inspiration, and education I needed to build the Elephant in the Room Men's Grooming Lounge.

STAYING POSITIVE IS A CHOICE

It's easy to be positive and happy when everything is going well, but my new found passion for life was going to be tested on a daily basis. I had to develop the ability to choose my perspective and how to avoid emotional reactions to adversity.

I knew I wanted Clay Clark my brother-in-law (former U.S. Small Business Administration Entrepreneur of the Year) to invest in me and to be both my partner and mentor in this new venture. However, at that time there was no name and the business was just an idea in my head. It was just a concept for the creation of a place where men could good to relax, and partake in an uplifting conversation while enjoying a tailored haircut. I want to point out that I was intentional about who I wanted to partner with, Clay was someone that had strengths in areas that were my weak spots just as my strengths may not be his.

FINDING MY MENTOR ONE REJECTION AT A TIME

It is important when building a company to ensure that you focus on creating a quality product or service that customers love first. Clay would create the systems, marketing, the pricing model and the overall business model, while I would create the ground level experience and overall concept. Every Sunday at family day I found myself bringing up this men's grooming concept to Clay. I brought it up so many times that I got his attention but he didn't respond the way I thought he would. I brought it up so much that he was to the point where actually threatened to ban me from his house if I brought it up again.

Now I want to point out a few things, my perspective on a haircut experience wasn't the same as his and I kept using the same approach when trying to explain it to him. Like most men Clay had grown to tolerate haircuts, they were more like a chore similar to taking the trash out once a week. Getting a haircut was not something that Clay enjoyed getting or discussing.

PERSISTENCE IS POWERFUL

Clay's previous haircut experiences consisted of being stuck in waiting room sitting on those blue plastic chairs recovered from a daycare while reading old "People" and "US Weekly Magazines" as the young boys next to him attempted not to throw another temper tantrum.

Clay was used to having stylists who reeked of cigarettes cutting his hair. He was used to having stylists who were passionate about sharing intimate details of their most recent failed relationship to an ex-convict. The haircuts he received ranged from poor to terrible and 50% of the time his hairstyle requests were not accommodated while receiving the haircut. Because I knew that Clay was not understanding what I was saying, I decided not to give up but to change my approach to pitching him.

GETTING CLAY'S ATTENTION

I knew that Clay paid his kids to massage his hands or to give him an actual scalp massage, so I knew that if presented correctly he too would see the value that a high-quality men's grooming lounge could provide to men. One Sunday while at family day, Clay was sitting on the couch while watching his favorite football team (the New England Patriots) play. Little did he know, but I had prepared my presentation was ready to go.

When it came time for the kids to give him his scalp massage I told them I had this covered, I proceeded to start with a hot towel and placed it on his face. Second I had him inhale a peppermint oil blend as I massaged his scalp. As the peppermint oil was setting in and the cool calming effect was taking place I removed the hot towel and applied a face moisturizer to his face. As I was finishing I mentioned that this is part of what my men's grooming lounge was going to offer to their customers. At that moment he started believing in the idea and wanted to know more. The next challenge was getting him to believe in me. That started a 2-year long journey.

LEARN TO RISE AND GRIND

I took me two years to earn Clay's respect and trust. I worked side by side with him and assisted him in launching 2 other businesses. During this time of working with Clay, I saw him set his alarm for 4:00 AM every day. I saw him make his to-do lists every day and I saw him put in the grind needed to create the success he achieved.

After two years of getting up early, making to-do-lists, walking fast and working with him I realized that he was a confident person because he made daily small commitments to himself and that he actually honored those commitments.

Rather than feeling dissonance as a result of setting goals and not completing them he actually was becoming a progressively more confident person every week I shadowed him. I started realizing that as a result of getting up at the same time as him, making my daily to-do lists and living a purposeful life I too was becoming a more confident person. I also realized that he was becoming more confident in me as a result of the consistent work-ethic that I was demonstrating on a daily basis.

UNANSWERED QUESTIONS

During this process, I had a lot of unanswered questions like:

- When would be we open our first men's grooming lounge?

- When would we find a location?

- Why are we spending time on all these other businesses when they have nothing to do with the Men's Grooming?

I chose to focus and learn from all the experiences that Clay was providing because I recognized that I was becoming a better person every day and he might just have a plan. After work each day I invested my time into doing hours and hours of extensive research and preparing myself for the opportunity for when he would say yes. I had to ensure that I was mentally and financially ready to take advantage of the trust that I had now built with my mentor. Then one day it happened.

Clay told me that he would match me dollar for dollar when it came to investing in the men's grooming lounge and that he would provide the physical space

Want to own your own business? Learn more about franchise opportunities at www.EITRLounge.com

11

for our first location. He told me he would supply the marketing, the systems and he even supplied the name, Elephant In The Room Men's Grooming Lounge.

I WISH I KNEW THEN WHAT I KNOW NOW.

Have you ever looked back in life and said, "I wish I knew then what I know now"?

The game-changing life lessons that we all learn along the way can either come about as a result of painful mistakes or as a result of learning from mentors.

However, to help you avoid some of the pain that I have experienced along the way in route to building The Elephant In The Room Men's Grooming Lounge I have compiled what I believe to be some of the most insightful and impactful lessons, quotes, and knowledge that every man needs to know to become successful.

SHOULD WE PAY FOR THE FOOD OR THE LIGHT BILL?

I remember growing up in a family where we struggled to pay rent each month. We had to decide whether to keep the lights on or to have food to eat. My parents were intentional about making sure that my sister and I went to public schools in districts with average higher income and I now understand why. Growing up, many of my friends' parents were doctors, lawyers, and business owners. Most of the time, my friends' mothers didn't have to work unless they wanted to.

INGRAINING THE SUCCESS MINDSET

As a kid, it appeared to me that my friends were somehow already ingrained with the mindset that they too would become successful. I didn't realize this until later in life, but their mindset was created because it was taught to them by their parents that this level of success in life was normal. My friends didn't know anything else. These kids who grew up in high income earning families are the kids who grew up to make more money than the average American. These kids grew up to live in houses that were bigger than the houses of the average American.

These kids grew up to be adults who sent their kids to private schools if they wanted to. These kids grew up to travel several times a year. To these kids all of this was normal. Intentionally or unintentionally, the parents of my friends instilled in their kids the mindset of achieving a level of success as a result of their overall work ethic and mindset.

26 BECOMING AN ENTREPRENEUR AT THE AGE OF 26

My journey as an entrepreneur started when I was 26 years old. It was at this time that I first realized that every action and every decision had gotten me to that exact moment in time. All of my decisions up until that point lead me to the type of relationships I had and to the level of financial success, I had not achieved. At that very specific moment in time, I decided to take control of my life and to change it for the better. My decision to change happened in a split second, but the results themselves took a little longer.

 ## BUILDING A NEW FOUNDATION

It was like bulldozing a structure to the ground and starting to rebuild it from the ground up. After much hard work, in less than 5 years, with Clay's help, we would go on to build a multi-million dollar brand that gave me the time freedom and financial freedom that I was searching for while teaching me the life lessons that I needed to know to become successful in the games of life.

LEARNING THE PROVEN PRINCIPLES

The same principles that we used to create the Elephant in the Room Men's Grooming Lounge brand are the same principles that every successful person uses to create their own success. For me, it was very important to be intentional about where I spent my time and who I spent my time with. I relentlessly focused on making sure to create a high-quality brand that would be would be viewed as being valuable by my ideal and likely buyers.

I focused on projecting to others the success that I knew I would someday achieve. Today I now realize that our thoughts are the deciding factor and that they ultimately make the difference.

THE 57 WORDS OF WISDOM

"In order for others to take you seriously you must first take yourself seriously."

– Justin Moore

(Co-founder of The Elephant in the Room Men's Grooming Lounge)

NOTABLE QUOTABLE
....

"Brand is just a perception, and perception will match reality over time. Sometimes it will be ahead, other times it will be behind. But brand is simply a collective impression some have about a product."

– Elon Musk

(The billionaire entrepreneur behind Tesla, SpaceX, PayPal, SolarCity, etc.)

Want to own your own business? Learn more about franchise opportunities at www.EITRLounge.com

17

"You know more about yourself than others do. Use this toward your advantage, don't speak of your doubts, shortcomings, weaknesses or insecurities."

– Clay Clark

(Former U.S. Small Business Administration Entrepreneur of the Year, the Co-Founder of The Elephant In The Room, Member of the Forbes Business Coach Council, and the host of iTunes chart-topping podcast, the Thrivetime Show)

NOTABLE QUOTABLE

"To know thyself is the beginning of wisdom."

- Socrates

(A classical Greek philosopher who was credited as being one of the founders of modern Western Philosophy)

3

"The best way to help yourself is to help others by inspiring, motivating and helping them to grow."

– Justin Moore

(Co-founder of The Elephant in the Room Men's Grooming Lounge)

NOTABLE QUOTABLE
....

"You will get all you want in life, if you help enough other people get what they want."

– Zig Ziglar

(Motivational speaker and New York Times best-selling author)

Want to own your own business? Learn more about franchise opportunities at www.EITRLounge.com

19

"Determine what are you preparing for. Know your goals, take aim and fire."

– Clay Clark

(Former U.S. Small Business Administration Entrepreneur of the Year, the Co-Founder of The Elephant In The Room, Member of the Forbes Business Coach Council, and the host of iTunes chart-topping podcast, the Thrivetime Show)

NOTABLE QUOTABLE

"There is one quality which one must possess to win, and that is definiteness of purpose, the knowledge of what one wants, and a burning desire to possess it."

– Napoleon Hill

(Best-selling author of Think and Grow Rich and the former speech writer to President Franklin Delano Roosevelt)

5

"To achieve your goal, your must have to have the mindset that you have already received it."

– Justin Moore

(Co-founder of The Elephant in the Room Men's Grooming Lounge)

NOTABLE QUOTABLE

"Genius is 1 percent inspiration, and 99 percent perspiration."

– Thomas Edison

(The legendary inventor whose team created the first practical light bulb, the first recorded audio, and the motion picture technology while creating General Electric)

Want to own your own business? Learn more about franchise opportunities at www.EITRLounge.com

21

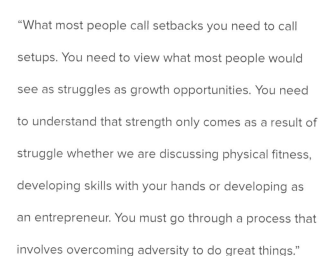

"What most people call setbacks you need to call setups. You need to view what most people would see as struggles as growth opportunities. You need to understand that strength only comes as a result of struggle whether we are discussing physical fitness, developing skills with your hands or developing as an entrepreneur. You must go through a process that involves overcoming adversity to do great things."

– Clay Clark

(Former U.S. Small Business Administration Entrepreneur of the Year, the Co-Founder of The Elephant In The Room, Member of the Forbes Business Coach Council, and the host of iTunes chart-topping podcast, the Thrivetime Show)

NOTABLE QUOTABLE

"Every setback is a setup for a comeback. God wants to bring you out better than you were before."

– Joel Osteen

(New York Times best-selling author and the Senior Pastor of Lakewood Christian Church in Houston, Texas)

7

"It's not so much about spending time doing the right things, as it is about not spending time doing the wrong things."

– Justin Moore

(Co-founder of The Elephant in the Room Men's Grooming Lounge)

NOTABLE QUOTABLE

"People think focus means saying yes to the thing you've got to focus on. But that's not what it means at all. It means saying no to the hundred other good ideas that there are. You have to pick carefully. I'm actually as proud of the things we haven't done as the things I have done. Innovation is saying no to 1,000 things."

– Steve Jobs

(The co-founder of Apple and the former CEO of PIXAR)

8

"Your time is yours to give. You choose to give your time no one has the ability take it."

– Clay Clark

(Former U.S. Small Business Administration Entrepreneur of the Year, the Co-Founder of The Elephant In The Room, Member of the Forbes Business Coach Council, and the host of iTunes chart-topping podcast, the Thrivetime Show)

NOTABLE QUOTABLE

"This is not about managing your time. It is about keeping Your whole life under control. Plan the life you want or live the life you don't want…"

– Lee Cockerell

(Former Executive Vice President of Walt Disney World Resorts who once managed 40,000 team members)

9

"The person who is asking questions is in control of the conversation."

– Justin Moore

(Co-founder of The Elephant in the Room Men's Grooming Lounge)

NOTABLE QUOTABLE

"You don't need a big close as many sales reps believe. You risk losing your customer when you save all the good stuff to the end. Keep the customer actively involved throughout the presentation and watch your results improve."

– Harvey Mackay

(New York Times best-selling author and iconic sales trainer)

"You will fall to the level of preparation, the notion that you will rise to the occasion is false. Those who fail to prepare will lose."

– Clay Clark

(Former U.S. Small Business Administration Entrepreneur of the Year, the Co-Founder of The Elephant In The Room, Member of the Forbes Business Coach Council, and the host of iTunes chart-topping podcast, the Thrivetime Show)

NOTABLE QUOTABLE

"My personal coaching philosophy, my mentality, has always been to make things as difficult as possible for players in practice, however bad we can make them, I make them."

– Bill Belichick

(Legendary NFL football coach of the New England Patriots)

11

"The decisions to change takes a split second, it is the process that takes time. It's like this with all things. You must embrace the process."

– Justin Moore

(Co-founder of The Elephant in the Room Men's Grooming Lounge)

NOTABLE QUOTABLE

"Transformation is a process, and as life happens there are tons of ups and downs. It's a journey of discovery – there are moments on mountaintops and moments in deep valleys of despair."

– Rick Warren

(The New York Times best-selling author, founder and senior pastor of Saddleback Church, an evangelical megachurch in Lake Forest, California, that is the eighth-largest church in the United States)

Want to own your own business? Learn more about franchise opportunities at www.EITRLounge.com

27

"The words we speak and hear can impact us either negatively or positively. For every word taken in from the environment around you that is negative, you must counterbalance it with three positive words."

– Clay Clark

(Former U.S. Small Business Administration Entrepreneur of the Year, the Co-Founder of The Elephant In The Room, Member of the Forbes Business Coach Council, and the host of iTunes chart-topping podcast, the Thrivetime Show)

NOTABLE QUOTABLE

"Don't wait until everything is just right. It will never be perfect. There will always be challenges, obstacles, and less than perfect conditions. So what? Get started now. With each step you take, you will grow stronger and stronger, more and more skilled, more and more self-confident, and more and more successful."

- Mark Victor Hansen

(The best-selling author behind the Chicken Soup for the Soul series of books)

"Think it, write it, and speak it into existence."

– Justin Moore

(Co-founder of The Elephant in the Room Men's Grooming Lounge)

NOTABLE QUOTABLE

"Setting goals is the first step in turning the invisible into the visible."

– Tony Robbins

(New York Time best-selling author and motivational expert.)

14

"30 day goal: Look in the mirror every morning and every evening and say; "I am happy, healthy, whole, blessed and successful" ten times."

– Clay Clark

(Former U.S. Small Business Administration Entrepreneur of the Year, the Co-Founder of The Elephant In The Room, Member of the Forbes Business Coach Council, and the host of iTunes chart-topping podcast, the Thrivetime Show)

NOTABLE QUOTABLE
....

"If you can dream it, you can do it."

– Walt Disney

(The famous co-founder of the Disney Empire who lost it all financially multiple times before finally achieving success with the Disney company)

15

"Is not so much about making others believe in you as it is making your subconscious a believer."

– Justin Moore

(Co-founder of The Elephant in the Room Men's Grooming Lounge)

NOTABLE QUOTABLE
....

"Winners never quit, and quitters never win."

– Vince Lombardi

(The football player, coach, and executive in the National Football League (NFL). He is best known as the head coach of the Green Bay Packers during the 1960s, where he led the team to three straight and five total NFL Championships in seven years, in addition to winning the first two Super Bowls at the conclusion of the 1966 and 1967 NFL seasons.)

16

"You will become the average of the people that you choose to spend the most time with."

– Clay Clark

(Former U.S. Small Business Administration Entrepreneur of the Year, the Co-Founder of The Elephant In The Room, Member of the Forbes Business Coach Council, and the host of iTunes chart-topping podcast, the Thrivetime Show)

NOTABLE QUOTABLE

. . . .

"You are the average of the five people you associate with."

– Tim Ferriss

(The New York Times best-selling author of The Four Hour Work Week)

17

"Don't use weak words. Don't say 'kind of', 'sort of' or 'maybe.' Speak power words such as 'definitely,' 'I am in 100% agreement,' or 'I will do get it done.'"

– Justin Moore

(Co-founder of The Elephant in the Room Men's Grooming Lounge)

NOTABLE QUOTABLE

"Think twice before you speak, because your words and influence will plant the seed of either success or failure in the mind of another."

– Napoleon Hill

(The best-selling author of Think and Grow Rich)

Want to own your own business? Learn more about franchise opportunities at www.EITRLounge.com

33

18

"Be early and honor your commitments, this will be your character and at times it may be the only and most valuable thing you have."

– Clay Clark

(Former U.S. Small Business Administration Entrepreneur of the Year, the Co-Founder of The Elephant In The Room, Member of the Forbes Business Coach Council, and the host of iTunes chart-topping podcast, the Thrivetime Show)

NOTABLE QUOTABLE

"A man has no right to occupy another man's time unnecessarily."

– John D. Rockefeller

(The son of a con artist who had to begin working at the age of 16 to support his family because his father abandoned his family)

"Priorities: Support yourself before you look to support anyone else. The government isn't that support line, you should support them."

– Justin Moore

(Co-founder of The Elephant in the Room Men's Grooming Lounge)

NOTABLE QUOTABLE

· ·

"You cannot help men permanently by doing for them what they could and should do for themselves."

– Abraham Lincoln

(The 16th President of the United States who helped to end slavery in America)

"Be early and hold to your commitments, this will be your character and at times it may be the only and most valuable thing you have."

– Clay Clark

(Former U.S. Small Business Administration Entrepreneur of the Year, the Co-Founder of The Elephant In The Room, Member of the Forbes Business Coach Council, and the host of iTunes chart-topping podcast, the Thrivetime Show)

NOTABLE QUOTABLE

"Every day we have plenty of opportunities to get angry, stressed or offended. But what you're doing when you indulge these negative emotions is giving something outside yourself power over your happiness. You can choose to not let little things upset you."

– Joel Osteen

(New York Times best-selling author and one of America's most well known pastors)

21

"Social media never attach your name to something negative. Keep negative emotions and feelings out of social media posts and emails. Social media is a tool to judge someone's character and morals."

– Justin Moore

(Co-founder of The Elephant in the Room Men's Grooming Lounge)

NOTABLE QUOTABLE

"If you must speak ill of another, do not speak it, write it in the sand near the water's edge."

– Napoleon Hill

(The best-selling author of Think and Grow Rich and the father of the modern self-help movement)

"If you personally lend someone money to help them out assume that you will never get it back. If you agree to lend someone money write up an agreement with details, the loan amount, the interest rate, and the payment amounts. Even with those circumstances I wish you good luck when it comes to collecting what you are owed."

– Clay Clark

(Former U.S. Small Business Administration Entrepreneur of the Year, the Co-Founder of The Elephant In The Room, Member of the Forbes Business Coach Council, and the host of iTunes chart-topping podcast, the Thrivetime Show)

NOTABLE QUOTABLE
....

"If thou wilt lend this money, lend it not as to thy friends; for when did friendship take a breed of barren metal of his friend? But lend it rather to thine enemy; Who, if he break, thou mayest with better face exact the penalty."

– William Shakespeare

(The famous playwright)

23

"Never carry a monthly balance on a credit card. Don't be a slave to the lender."

– Justin Moore

(Co-founder of The Elephant in the Room Men's Grooming Lounge)

NOTABLE QUOTABLE

"Act your wage."

– Dave Ramsey

(New York Times best-selling author and national radio talk show host)

Want to own your own business? Learn more about franchise opportunities at www.EITRLounge.com

39

"Save 10% of your income."

– Clay Clark

(Former U.S. Small Business Administration Entrepreneur
of the Year, the Co-Founder of The Elephant In The Room,
Member of the Forbes Business Coach Council, and the
host of iTunes chart-topping podcast, the Thrivetime Show)

NOTABLE QUOTABLE

"If you cannot save money, the seeds
of greatness are not in you."

– W. Clement Stone

(The legendary best-selling author and motivational speaker)

25

"If you are not willing to work, nothing will work."

– Justin Moore

(Co-founder of The Elephant in the Room Men's Grooming Lounge)

NOTABLE QUOTABLE

"And where I excel is ridiculous, sickening, work ethic. You know, while the other guy's sleeping? I'm working."

– Will Smith

(Smith has been nominated for five Golden Globe Awards and two Academy Awards, and has won four Grammy Awards.)

Want to own your own business? Learn more about franchise opportunities at www.EITRLounge.com

41

On
On
On

On

26

"This world and the people in it owe you nothing, you must go and earn it."

– Clay Clark

(Former U.S. Small Business Administration Entrepreneur of the Year, the Co-Founder of The Elephant In The Room, Member of the Forbes Business Coach Council, and the host of iTunes chart-topping podcast, the Thrivetime Show)

NOTABLE QUOTABLE
....

"Excellence is being able to perform at a high level over and over again. You can hit a half-court shot once. That's just the luck of the draw. If you consistently do it... that's excellence."

– Jay-Z

(Originally known as Shawn Carter, he is one of the best-selling musicians of all time, having sold more than 100 million records, while receiving 21 Grammy Awards for his music)

27

"Don't be upset that someone has more than you. Just invest the time to asking yourself, how did they did do it? Ask yourself, why are they ahead of you? Then go and make the changes."

– Justin Moore
(Co-founder of The Elephant in the Room Men's Grooming Lounge)

NOTABLE QUOTABLE

"Rarely do we find men who willingly engage in hard, solid thinking. There is an almost universal quest for easy answers and half-baked solutions. Nothing pains some people more than having to think."

– Martin Luther King, Jr.
(The man and minister who was at the center of the Civil Rights Movement in America)

Want to own your own business? Learn more about franchise opportunities at www.EITRLounge.com

43

"The world is judging you based upon what you do and not what people say."

– Clay Clark

(Former U.S. Small Business Administration Entrepreneur of the Year, the Co-Founder of The Elephant In The Room, Member of the Forbes Business Coach Council, and the host of iTunes chart-topping podcast, the Thrivetime Show)

NOTABLE QUOTABLE

"There are four ways, and only four ways, in which we have contact with the world. We are evaluated and classified by these four contacts: what we do, how we look, what we say, and how we say it."

– Dale Carnegie

(Best-selling author of How to Win Friends and Influence People)

29

"Dress the part. Be prepared, looking the part is half the battle."

– Justin Moore

(Co-founder of The Elephant in the Room Men's Grooming Lounge)

NOTABLE QUOTABLE

"People should not judge a book by its cover, but they do and it will never change."

– Clay Clark

(Former U.S. Small Business Administration Entrepreneur of the Year, Co-founder of The Elephant in the Room Men's Grooming Lounge, Member of the Forbes Business Coach Council, and the host of the iTunes charts topping podcast, the Thrivetime Show)

Want to own your own business? Learn more about franchise opportunities at www.EITRLounge.com

45

"You can watch Ted Talks until you know everything the world has to teach you, but no one cares unless you get something done."

– Clay Clark

(Former U.S. Small Business Administration Entrepreneur of the Year, the Co-Founder of The Elephant In The Room, Member of the Forbes Business Coach Council, and the host of iTunes chart-topping podcast, the Thrivetime Show)

NOTABLE QUOTABLE

"Vision without execution is hallucination."

– Thomas Edison

(Legendary inventor of the modern light bulb, recorded sound and the founder of General Electric)

31

"To grow you have to leave some people behind, people finish the race at different times. Some people don't finish at all. Don't stop your race because others chose to stop there."

– Justin Moore

(Co-founder of The Elephant in the Room Men's Grooming Lounge)

NOTABLE QUOTABLE

"A few of the managers we spoke with for this book worried that the tour of duty framework might give employees "permission" to leave. But permission is not yours to give or to withhold, and believing you have that power is simply a self-deception that leads to a dishonest relationship with your employees. Employees don't need your permission to switch companies, and if you try to assert that right, they'll simply make their move behind your back."

– Reid Hoffman

(Founder of Linkedin)

 47

32

"Success doesn't care about your race, religion, or gender. If you believe otherwise you have given up."

– Clay Clark

(Former U.S. Small Business Administration Entrepreneur of the Year, the Co-Founder of The Elephant In The Room, Member of the Forbes Business Coach Council, and the host of iTunes chart-topping podcast, the Thrivetime Show)

NOTABLE QUOTABLE

"There are no secrets to success. It is the result of preparation, hard work, and learning from failure."

– Colin Powell

(A retired four-star general in the United States Army and the 65th United States Secretary of State)

33

"Control your emotions or someone else will. It takes more self-control to do what is not natural and what is right."

– Justin Moore

(Co-founder of The Elephant in the Room Men's Grooming Lounge)

NOTABLE QUOTABLE

....

"If you are not doing hard things, you are doing the right things."

– Lee Cockerell

(ThriveTimeShow.com Mentor and former Executive Vice President of Walt Disney World Resorts who once managed over 40,000 employees)

Want to own your own business? Learn more about franchise opportunities at www.EITRLounge.com

49

34

"Celebrate the victories of others and speak positively over them, don't resent or be jealous of their accomplishments, but be glad and excited."

– Clay Clark

(Former U.S. Small Business Administration Entrepreneur of the Year, the Co-Founder of The Elephant In The Room, Member of the Forbes Business Coach Council, and the host of iTunes chart-topping podcast, the Thrivetime Show)

NOTABLE QUOTABLE

"Surround yourself with only people who are going to lift you higher."

– Oprah Winfrey

(The teenage abuse and rape victim turned media mogul)

35

"Pay yourself first."

– Justin Moore

(Co-founder of The Elephant in the Room Men's Grooming Lounge)

NOTABLE QUOTABLE

"In fact, what determines your wealth is not how much you make but how much you keep of what you make."

– David Bach

(New York best-selling author of Automatic Millionaire)

Want to own your own business? Learn more about franchise opportunities at www.EITRLounge.com

51

36

"Take care of your health. Both your mind and your body must have ongoing exercise and stimulation or atrophy will occur."

– Clay Clark

(Former U.S. Small Business Administration Entrepreneur of the Year, the Co-Founder of The Elephant In The Room, Member of the Forbes Business Coach Council, and the host of iTunes chart-topping podcast, the Thrivetime Show)

NOTABLE QUOTABLE

"You either pay now or pay later with just about every decision you make about where and how you spend your time."

– Lee Cockerell

(The former Executive Vice President of Walt Disney World Resorts who once managed over 40,000 employees at the world's number tourist destination)

37

"Always respect a woman. That's someone's daughter, mother, sister, she is to be celebrated."

– Justin Moore

(Co-founder of The Elephant in the Room Men's Grooming Lounge)

NOTABLE QUOTABLE

"Husbands, love your wives just as Christ loved the church and gave himself up for her."

– Ephesians 5:25

(The Bible)

38

"Do you want to be liked or respected? If you want to be successful it will require the disapproval of people that you must hold accountable."

– Clay Clark

(Former U.S. Small Business Administration Entrepreneur of the Year, the Co-Founder of The Elephant In The Room, Member of the Forbes Business Coach Council, and the host of iTunes chart-topping podcast, the Thrivetime Show)

NOTABLE QUOTABLE

"Better to be feared than loved, if you cannot be both."

– Niccolo Machiavelli

(The famous Italian diplomat, historian and philosopher)

39

"Give compliments freely. Say please and thank you whenever possible. Verbal compliments are gifts."

– Justin Moore

(Co-founder of The Elephant in the Room Men's Grooming Lounge)

NOTABLE QUOTABLE
....

"I can live for two months on a good compliment."

– Mark Twain

(Best-selling American writer and entrepreneur whose novels include The Adventures of Tom Sawyer, its sequel the Adventures of Huckleberry Finn (1885) and "The Great American Novel".

Want to own your own business? Learn more about franchise opportunities at www.EITRLounge.com

55

"When in doubt be early, overdress and don't apologize. Excuses never matter and they never make a difference. No one ever made a million dollars by someone else feeling sorry for them."

– Clay Clark

(Former U.S. Small Business Administration Entrepreneur of the Year, the Co-Founder of The Elephant In The Room, Member of the Forbes Business Coach Council, and the host of iTunes chart-topping podcast, the Thrivetime Show)

NOTABLE QUOTABLE
....

"Before anything else, preparation is the key to success."

– Alexander Graham Bell

(A Scottish-born scientist and inventor who is credited with the inventing and patenting of the world's practical telephone and founding the American Telephone and Telegraph Company (AT&T) in 1885.)

"Wear clothes that fit and are appropriate. The difference in a professional rock star and you is that he gets paid to dress that way and you can't afford to dress that way."

– Justin Moore

(Co-founder of The Elephant in the Room Men's Grooming Lounge)

NOTABLE QUOTABLE

"We don't know where our first impressions come from or precisely what they mean, so we don't always appreciate their fragility."

– Malcolm Gladwell

(Best-selling author of The Tipping Point, Blink, Outliers, etc.)

42

"Create a win-win deal every time you create a deal."

– Clay Clark

(Former U.S. Small Business Administration Entrepreneur of the Year, the Co-Founder of The Elephant In The Room, Member of the Forbes Business Coach Council, and the host of iTunes chart-topping podcast, the Thrivetime Show)

NOTABLE QUOTABLE

"Look to create a win, don't just look at what benefits you. Win-win is a frame of mind and heart that constantly seeks mutual benefit in all human interactions. Win-win means agreements or solutions are mutually beneficial and satisfying. We both get to eat the pie, and it tastes pretty darn good!"

– Stephen Covey

(The best-selling author of The 7 Habits of Highly Effective People)

"If you consistently over deliver you will be overpaid. Your work ethic is yours.
You take your work ethic everywhere. Don't get fooled and allow yourself to feel under-appreciated or under paid. Working under what you're capable only hurts you and no one else."

– Justin Moore

(Co-founder of The Elephant in the Room Men's Grooming Lounge)

NOTABLE QUOTABLE

"Render more service than that for which you are being paid and you will soon be paid for more than you render."

– Napoleon Hill

(Best-selling author of Think and Grow Rich)

"You should always outwork your pay, this way you will alway be eligible for a raise."

– Clay Clark

(Former U.S. Small Business Administration Entrepreneur of the Year, the Co-Founder of The Elephant In The Room, Member of the Forbes Business Coach Council, and the host of iTunes chart-topping podcast, the Thrivetime Show)

NOTABLE QUOTABLE
....

"When you embrace the process of your work, instead of focusing on the results, you'll always be happier, plus you'll do a much better job."

– Russell Simmons

(The chair and CEO of Rush Communications who was the co-founder the iconic hip-hop music label Def Jam Recordings and the founder of the clothing fashion lines Phat Farm, Argyleculture, and Tantris. Simmons' net worth was estimated at $340 million as of 2011.)

43

"View yourself as a brand, that will be projected to the masses. How will you market yourself?

How will you be displayed? What is your value? Where is your placement?"

– Justin Moore

(Co-founder of The Elephant in the Room Men's Grooming Lounge)

NOTABLE QUOTABLE

"It takes 20 years to build a reputation and five minutes to ruin it. If you think about that, you'll do things differently."

– Warren Buffett

(The founder of Berkshire Hathaway and a man considered by many to be the best investor of his generation. Warren Buffett's portfolio of investments include: Coca Cola, GEICO, See's Candies, Bank of America, Omaha Furniture, etc.)

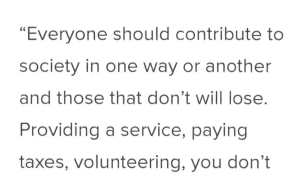

"Everyone should contribute to society in one way or another and those that don't will lose. Providing a service, paying taxes, volunteering, you don't get ahead by doing less."

– Clay Clark

(Former U.S. Small Business Administration Entrepreneur of the Year, the Co-Founder of The Elephant In The Room, Member of the Forbes Business Coach Council, and the host of iTunes chart-topping podcast, the Thrivetime Show)

NOTABLE QUOTABLE

"Lazy hands make for poverty, but diligent hands bring wealth."

– Proverbs 10:4

(The Bible)

45

"'I can't' should never be apart of your vocabulary. Replace 'I can't' with 'I am working on' or 'I am improving at.'"

— Justin Moore

(Co-founder of The Elephant in the Room Men's Grooming Lounge)

NOTABLE QUOTABLE
....

"Whatever the mind can conceive and believe, the mind can achieve."

— Napoleon Hill

(Best-selling self-help author of all-time and the former personal apprentice for Andrew Carnegie)

Want to own your own business? Learn more about franchise opportunities at www.EITRLounge.com

63

"Don't spend what you don't have, budget for unseen expenses and this will help give you peace of mind."

– Clay Clark

(Former U.S. Small Business Administration Entrepreneur of the Year, the Co-Founder of The Elephant In The Room, Member of the Forbes Business Coach Council, and the host of iTunes chart-topping podcast, the Thrivetime Show)

NOTABLE QUOTABLE
....

"Act your wage."

– Dave Ramsey

(Personal financial planning guru, New York Times best-selling author and national radio talk show host)

47

"Ideas don't matter. It's the execution of those ideas that matters."

– Justin Moore

(Co-founder of The Elephant in the Room Men's Grooming Lounge)

NOTABLE QUOTABLE

"Discipline is the bridge between having goals and achieving those goals. Very few people ever achieve those goals because their number one goal is to be at peace with everybody including the doubters, the competition, and people that want to see them fail. To me, I see the peace sign as a trigger and a middle finger. I will not lose because I choose to diligently execute ethical business systems while running over any negative people along the way."

– Clay Clark

(Former U.S. Small Business Administration Entrepreneur of the Year, the Co-Founder of The Elephant In The Room, Member of the Forbes Business Coach Council, and the host of iTunes chart-topping podcast, the Thrivetime Show)

"Live below your means."

– Clay Clark

(Former U.S. Small Business Administration Entrepreneur
of the Year, the Co-Founder of The Elephant In The Room,
Member of the Forbes Business Coach Council, and the
host of iTunes chart-topping podcast, the Thrivetime Show)

NOTABLE QUOTABLE

"Act your wage."

– Dave Ramsey

*(Personal financial planning guru, New York Times best-
selling author and national radio talk show host)*

49

"Will you do what's required of you to get the results you want? Seldom will you see someone that will sacrifice and put this principle into action but most people will speak of their desire for success."

– Justin Moore

(Co-founder of The Elephant in the Room Men's Grooming Lounge)

NOTABLE QUOTABLE

"Just work like hell. You just have to put in 80 to 100 hour weeks every week. If other people are putting in 40 hour workweeks and you're putting in 100 hour workweeks, then even if you're doing the same thing … you will achieve in four months what it takes them a year to achieve."

– Elon Musk

(The billionaire entrepreneur behind Tesla, SpaceX, PayPal, SolarCity, etc.)

"Look to serve others and in return you will be served."

– Clay Clark

(Former U.S. Small Business Administration Entrepreneur of the Year, the Co-Founder of The Elephant In The Room, Member of the Forbes Business Coach Council, and the host of iTunes chart-topping podcast, the Thrivetime Show)

NOTABLE QUOTABLE

"Successful people are always looking for opportunities to help others. Unsuccessful people are always asking, What's in it for me?"

– Brian Tracy

(The New York Times best-selling author and world-renowned sales guru)

51

"Those around you could not care about less how you feel, speak of nothing unless it's positive. What the mind can conceive it can achieve. If you think positive or negative you are right either way."

— **Justin Moore**

(Co-founder of The Elephant in the Room Men's Grooming Lounge)

NOTABLE QUOTABLE
....

"Success seems to be connected with action. Successful people keep moving. They make mistakes, but they don't quit."

— **Conrad Hilton**

(The legendary founder of the Hilton Hotel and Resort chain)

"Always portray trust, confidence, professionalism in the eyes of others. You can achieve this by the way you speak of others when they aren't around and by keeping your word."

– Clay Clark

(Former U.S. Small Business Administration Entrepreneur of the Year, the Co-Founder of The Elephant In The Room, Member of the Forbes Business Coach Council, and the host of iTunes chart-topping podcast, the Thrivetime Show)

NOTABLE QUOTABLE

"It takes 20 years to build a reputation and five minutes to ruin it. If you think about that, you'll do things differently."

– Warren Buffett

(The founder of Berkshire Hathaway who is regarded by many as the most successful investor in American history)

53

"Results Driven: Actions speak louder than words. Look at results, they are the best judgment of a person's character."

– Justin Moore

(Co-founder of The Elephant in the Room Men's Grooming Lounge)

NOTABLE QUOTABLE

"Character is like a tree and reputation like a shadow. The shadow is what we think of it; the tree is the real thing."

– Benjamin Franklin

(An American polymath who was one of the Founding Fathers of the United States. During his time, Benjamin Franklin was a renowned author, politician, scientist, inventor and diplomat. He alone convinced the French to supply the United States with the ammunitions and weapons needed to win the war against the British as the colonists faced certain defeat without the French support.)

Want to own your own business? Learn more about franchise opportunities at www.EITRLounge.com

71

54

"Focus on becoming a quality person with the hope that you will eventually find another whole person."

– Clay Clark

(Former U.S. Small Business Administration Entrepreneur of the Year, the Co-Founder of The Elephant In The Room, Member of the Forbes Business Coach Council, and the host of iTunes chart-topping podcast, the Thrivetime Show)

NOTABLE QUOTABLE
....

"Always do your best. What you plant now, you will harvest later."

– Og Mandino

(New York Times best-selling author and thought leader)

55

"Believe you will succeed.

Doubt is the enemy of faith."

– Justin Moore

*(Co-founder of The Elephant in the
Room Men's Grooming Lounge)*

NOTABLE QUOTABLE

"Whether you think you can, or you
think you can't–you're right."

– Henry Ford

*(The man who transformed the automobile industry with his
refinement of the assembly line system of manufacturing)*

Want to own your own business? Learn more about franchise opportunities at www.EITRLounge.com

73

56

"At the very core of everyman he wants to be an independent provider and leader, don't deny yourself of this."

– Clay Clark

(Former U.S. Small Business Administration Entrepreneur of the Year, the Co-Founder of The Elephant In The Room, Member of the Forbes Business Coach Council, and the host of iTunes chart-topping podcast, the Thrivetime Show)

NOTABLE QUOTABLE

"Nothing can stop the man with the right mental attitude from achieving his goal; nothing on earth can help the man with the wrong mental attitude."

– Thomas Jefferson

(One of the Founding Fathers of the United States)

57

"Learn new skills while you pay the bills. The world will gladly and only pay for the problems that you can conveniently solve."

– Justin Moore

(Co-founder of The Elephant in the Room Men's Grooming Lounge)

NOTABLE QUOTABLE

Education is the key to unlock the golden door of freedom."

– George Washington Carver

(The famous botanist who was born a slave and went on to completely revolutionize the way Americans farm)

Want to own your own business? Learn more about franchise opportunities at www.EITRLounge.com

75

CPSIA information can be obtained
at www.ICGtesting.com
Printed in the USA
FFHW012016130119
50070283-54898FF